French Dialogues for Beginners
Book 2

Over 100 Daily Used Phrases and Short Stories to Learn French in Your Car. Have Fun and Grow Your Vocabulary with Crazy Effective Language Learning Lessons

www.LearnLikeNatives.com

TABLE OF CONTENT

INTRODUCTION

Before we dive into some French, I want to congratulate you, whether you're just beginning, continuing, or resuming your language learning journey. Here at Learn Like a Native, we understand the determination it takes to pick up a new language and after reading this book, you'll be another step closer to achieving your language goals. As a thank you for learning with us, we are giving you free access to our 'Speak Like a Native' eBook. It's packed full of practical advice and insider tips on how to make language learning quick, easy, and most importantly, enjoyable. Head over to LearnLikeNatives.com to access your free guide and peruse our huge selection of language learning resources.

Learning a new language is a bit like cooking—you need several different ingredients and the right technique, but the end result is sure to be delicious. We created this book of short stories for learning French because language is alive. Language is about the senses—hearing, tasting the words on your tongue, and touching another culture up close. Learning a language in a classroom is a fine place to start, but it's not a complete introduction to a language.

In this book, you'll find a language come to life. These short stories are miniature immersions into the French language, at a level that is perfect for beginners. This book is not a lecture on grammar. It's not an endless vocabulary list. This book is the closest you can come to a language immersion without leaving the country. In the stories within, you will see people speaking to each other, going through daily life situations, and using the most common, helpful words and phrases in language.

You are holding the key to bringing your French studies to life.

Made for Beginners

We made this book with beginners in mind. You'll find that the language is simple, but not boring. Most of the book is in the present tense, so you will be able to focus on dialogues, root verbs, and understand and find patterns in subject-verb agreement.

This is not "just" a translated book. While reading novels and short stories translated into French is a wonderful thing, beginners (and even novices) often run into difficulty. Literary licenses and complex sentence structure can make reading in your second language truly difficult—not to mention BORING. That's why French Short Stories for Beginners is the perfect book to pick up. The stories are simple, but not infantile. They were not written for children, but the language is simple so that beginners can pick it up.

The Benefits of Learning a Second Language

If you have picked up this book, it's likely that you are already aware of the many benefits of learning a second language. Besides just being fun, knowing more than one language opens up a whole new world to you. You will be able to communicate with a much larger chunk of the world. Opportunities in the workforce will open up, and maybe even your day-to-day work will be improved. Improved communication can also help you expand your business. And from a neurological perspective, learning a second language is like taking your daily vitamins and eating well, for your brain!

How To Use The Book

The chapters of this book all follow the same structure:

- A short story with several dialogs
- A summary in French
- A list of important words and phrases and their English translation
- Questions to test your understanding
- Answers to check if you were right
- The English translation of the story to clear every doubt

You may use this book however is comfortable for you, but we have a few recommendations for getting the most out of the experience. Try these tips and if they work for you, you can use them on every chapter throughout the book.

1) Start by reading the story all the way through. Don't stop or get hung up on any particular words or phrases. See how much of the plot you can understand in this way. We think you'll get a lot more of it than you may expect, but it is completely normal not to understand everything in the story. You are learning a new language, and that takes time.

2) Read the summary in French. See if it matches what you have understood of the plot.

3) Read the story through again, slower this time. See if you can pick up the meaning of any words or phrases you don't understand by using context clues and the information from the summary.

4) Test yourself! Try to answer the five comprehension questions that come at the end of each story. Write your answers

down, and then check them against the answer key. How did you do? If you didn't get them all, no worries!

5) Look over the vocabulary list that accompanies the chapter. Are any of these the words you did not understand? Did you already know the meaning of some of them from your reading?

6) Now go through the story once more. Pay attention this time to the words and phrases you haven't understand. If you'd like, take the time to look them up to expand your meaning of the story. Every time you read over the story, you'll understand more and more.

7) Move on to the next chapter when you are ready.

Read and Listen

The audio version is the best way to experience this book, as you will hear a native French speaker tell you each story. You will become accustomed to their accent as you listen along, a huge plus for when you want to apply your new language skills in the real world.

If this has ignited your language learning passion and you are keen to find out what other resources are available, go to LearnLikeNatives.com, where you can access our vast range of free learning materials. Don't know where to begin? An excellent place to start is our 'Speak Like a Native' free eBook, full of practical advice and insider tips on how to make language learning quick, easy, and most importantly, enjoyable.

And remember, small steps add up to great advancements! No moment is better to begin learning than the present.

FREE BOOK!

Get the *FREE BOOK* that reveals the secrets path to learn any language fast, and without leaving your country.

Discover:

- The language 5 golden rules to master languages at will

- Proven mind training techniques to revolutionize your learning

- A complete step-by-step guide to conquering any language

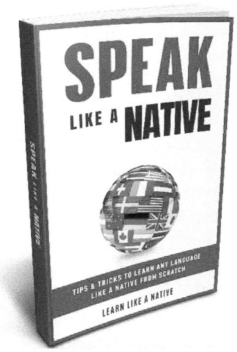

CHAPTER 1
John's Homework / School
+ Classroom

HISTOIRE

Mme Kloss est **enseignante** de quatrième année. Elle enseigne à l'école primaire Homewood. L'**école**

est dans un bâtiment en brique rouge. Elle est située dans une petite ville.

Mme Kloss a une **classe** de 15 élèves. Ses **élèves** sont des garçons et des filles. Ce sont habituellement de bons élèves. Mme Kloss a une habitude : ses élèves commencent la journée à leur **bureau**, assis sur leur **chaise**. Mme Kloss fait l'**appel**.

« Louise? », dit-elle.

« Ici! », s'écrie Louise.

« Mike? », dit Mme Kloss.

« Présent », dit Mike.

« John ? »

« Ici, madame Kloss », dit John.

Et ainsi de suite. Après l'appel, Mme Kloss commence la journée avec les **mathématiques**. Pour ses élèves, les mathématiques sont difficiles. La classe écoute Mme Kloss enseigner. Ils la regardent écrire au **tableau**. Parfois, un élève résout un problème devant la classe. Ils utilisent une **craie** pour écrire la solution. Les autres élèves font les problèmes dans leurs **cahiers**.

L'heure préférée de tout le monde est l'heure du déjeuner. Les élèves se rendent dans la cantine. Ils ont deux choix. L'un d'eux est un repas sain, de la viande et des légumes. L'autre choix est de la pizza ou des hamburgers. Certains élèves apportent un repas fait maison.

L'après-midi, ils étudient l'**histoire**. Le vendredi, ils ont des cours de **sciences** en **laboratoire**. Ils font des **expériences**, comme cultiver des plantes à partir d'un morceau de pomme de terre.

Mme Kloss donne des **devoirs** à ses élèves tous les jours. Ils ramènent le travail à la maison. Ils travaillent le soir. Le lendemain, ils l'amènent à l'école. La seule excuse pour ne pas avoir fait ses devoirs est un mot de leurs parents.

Un jour, la classe passe en revue les devoirs d'**anglais** ensemble.

« Tout le monde, apportez vos **papiers** à mon bureau », dit Mme Kloss. Tout le monde apporte ses devoirs à Mme Kloss. Tout le monde sauf John.

« John, où sont tes devoirs? », dit Mme Kloss.

Le visage de John est très rouge. Il est nerveux.

« Je ne les ai pas, dit John.

- As-tu un mot de tes parents? demande Mme Kloss.

- Non », dit John.

« Pourquoi n'avez-vous pas fait vos devoirs, alors? » demande Mme Kloss. John dit quelque chose très bas.

« Quoi? Nous ne t'entendons pas », dit Mme Kloss. Elle sourit gentiment à John. Il a l'air nerveux.

« Mon chien a mangé mes devoirs », dit John. Mme Kloss et les autres élèves rient. Cette excuse est l'excuse la plus typique pour ne pas avoir fait son travail.

« Est-ce dans ton **sac à dos**? Ou peut-être dans ton **casier**? » demande Mme Kloss. Elle veut aider John.

« Non, mon chien l'a mangé, insiste John.

- C'est **la plus vieille excuse du monde**, dit Mme Kloss.

- C'est vrai! », dit John. John est un bon élève. Il a habituellement de **bonnes notes**. Mme Kloss ne veut pas envoyer Jon dans le **bureau du directeur** pour avoir menti. Elle ne croit pas John, mais elle décide de lui donner une autre chance.

« Apporte-moi tes devoirs demain, dit Mme Kloss, voici une autre copie. » John prend la **feuille de travail** et remercie Mme Kloss. Les élèves se tournent vers leur cahier d'**art**. Aujourd'hui, en classe d'art, ils dessinent une image avec des **crayons** de couleur. Les élèves adorent les cours d'art. C'est l'occasion de se détendre. Ils dessinent et dessinent jusqu'à ce que la **cloche** sonne. L'école est terminée.

Les élèves parlent dans les couloirs. Ils échangent des mots. Les élèves de 4e année attendent à l'extérieur. Leurs parents viennent les chercher. Certains d'entre eux rentrent à pied. Certains d'entre eux sont en voiture. Les enseignants les aident à retrouver leurs parents.

Mme Kloss termine son travail. Elle range son **ordinateur portable** dans son sac. Sa salle de classe est propre et vide. Elle sort. Alors qu'elle se marche vers sa voiture, elle voit John et son père. Le père de John vient le chercher avec leur chien. Mme Kloss fait signe à John et à son père.

« Bonjour, John! dit Mme Kloss.

« Bonjour, madame Kloss », dit John.

« Est-ce le chien qui a mangé tes devoirs? », demande Mme Kloss. Elle sourit, donc John sait qu'elle se moque de lui.

« Oui, madame Kloss, dit le père de John. Merci de votre compréhension. John est tellement inquiet d'avoir des ennuis! »

Mme Kloss est stupéfaite! Cette fois, le chien a vraiment mangé les devoirs.

Liste de Vocabulaire

teacher	enseignant
school	école
class	classe
students	élèves
desk	bureau
chair	président
roll call	appel
math	mathématiques
blackboard	tableau noir
chalk	craie
notebook	carnet
history	histoire
science	science
lab	laboratoire
experiment	expérience

homework	devoirs
English	anglais
papers	documents
backpack	sac à dos
locker	casier
the oldest excuse in the book	la plus vieille excuse
straight A's	de bonnes notes
principal's office	bureau du directeur
worksheet	feuille de travail
pencils	crayons
bell	cloche
laptop	ordinateur portable

QUESTIONS

1) Comment commence la journée dans la classe de Mme Kloss?

    a) les élèves se lèvent et crient

    b) avec un devoir

    c) avec l'appel

    d) avec les cris de Mme Kloss

2) Quel est le moment de la journée préféré de tout le monde à l'école primaire Homewood?

    a) l'appel

    b) l'heure du repas

    c) le cours de mathématiques

    d) après la sonnerie

3) Pourquoi Mme Kloss dit-elle que l'excuse de John est la plus ancienne du livre?

a) parce que tout le monde utilise cette excuse

b) John est le plus âgé de la classe.

c) il a oublié son livre

d) son chien a sept ans

4) Que devez-vous avoir si vous ne faites pas vos devoirs?

a) une expérience scientifique

b) une bonne excuse

c) rien, il n'y a pas de problème

d) un mot de tes parents

5) Pourquoi Mme Kloss est-elle surprise à la fin de l'histoire?

a) elle réalise que John disait la vérité

b) le chien de John est en fait un cheval

c) John ne lui parle pas

d) le père de John ressemble à John

RÉPONSES

1) Comment commence la journée dans la classe de Mme Kloss?

    c) avec l'appel

2) Quel est le moment de la journée préféré de tout le monde à l'école primaire Homewood?

    b) l'heure du repas

3) Pourquoi Mme Kloss dit-elle que l'excuse de John est la plus ancienne du livre?

a) parce que tout le monde utilise cette excuse

4) Que devez-vous avoir si vous ne faites pas vos devoirs?

d) un mot de tes parents

5) Pourquoi Mme Kloss est-elle surprise à la fin de l'histoire?

a) elle réalise que John disait la vérité

Translation of the Story

John's Homework

STORY

Mrs. Kloss is a grade 4 **teacher**. She teaches at Homewood Elementary School. The **school** is in a red brick building. It is in a small town.

Mrs. Kloss has a **class** of 15 students. Her **students** are boys and girls. They are usually good students. Mrs. Kloss has a routine. Her students start the day at their **desks**, seated in their **chairs**. Mrs. Kloss calls **roll call**.

"Louise?" she says.

"Here!" shouts Louise.

31

"Mike?" says Mrs. Kloss.

"Present," says Mike.

"John?"

"Here, Mrs. Kloss," John says.

And so on. After roll call, Mrs. Kloss starts the day with **math**. For her students, math is difficult. The class listens to Mrs. Kloss teach. They watch as she writes on the **blackboard**. Sometimes, one student solves a problem in front of the class. They use **chalk** to write out the solution. The other students do the problems in their **notebooks**.

Everyone's favorite time is lunch time. The class goes to the lunchroom. They have two choices. One choice is a healthy meal of meat and vegetables. The other choice is pizza or hamburgers. Some students bring a lunch from home.

In the afternoon, they study **history**. On Fridays, they have **science** class in the **lab**. They do **experiments**, like growing plants from a piece of potato.

Mrs. Kloss gives her students **homework** every day. They take the work home. They work at night. The next day, they bring it to school. The only excuse for incomplete homework is a note from their parents.

One day, the class reviews the **English** homework together.

"Everyone, please bring your **papers** to my desk," says Mrs. Kloss. Everyone brings their homework to Mrs. Kloss. Everyone except for John.

"John, where is your homework?" says Mrs. Kloss.

John's face is very red. He is nervous.

"I don't have it," says John.

"Do you have a note from your parents?" asks Mrs. Kloss.

"No," says John.

"Why didn't you do your homework, then?" asks Mrs. Kloss. John says something very quietly.

"What? We can't hear you," says Mrs. Kloss. She gives John a kind smile. He looks nervous.

"My dog ate my homework," says John. Mrs. Kloss and the other students laugh. This excuse is the most typical excuse for not having work done.

"Is it in your **backpack**? Or maybe your **locker**?" asks Mrs. Kloss. She wants to help John.

"No, my dog ate it!" insists John.

"That's the **oldest excuse in the book**," says Mrs. Kloss.

"It is true!" says John. John is a good student. He usually makes **straight A's**. Mrs. Kloss does not want to send Jon to the **principal's office** for lying. She does not believe John, but she decides to give him another chance.

"Bring the homework tomorrow," says Mrs. Kloss. "Here is another copy." John takes the **worksheet** and thanks Mrs. Kloss. The class turns to their **art** notebook. Today in art class they are drawing a picture with colored **pencils**. Students love art class. It is a chance to relax. They draw and draw until the **bell** rings. School is over.

Students talk in the hallways. They exchange notes. The Grade 4 students wait outside. Their parents pick them up. Some of them are on foot. Some of them are in cars. The teachers help them to find their parents.

Mrs. Kloss finishes her work. She packs her **laptop** into her bag. Her classroom is clean and empty. She goes outside. As she walks to her car, she see John and his dad. John's father picks him up with their dog. Mrs. Kloss waves to John and his father.

"Hello, John!" says Mrs. Kloss.

"Good afternoon, Mrs. Kloss," John says.

"Is this the dog that ate your homework?" asks Mrs. Kloss. She smiles, so John knows she is teasing.

"Yes, Mrs. Kloss," says John's father. "Thank you for understanding. John is so worried about getting in trouble!"

Mrs. Kloss is shocked! This time, the dog really did eat the homework.

CHAPTER 2
Thrift Store Bargain / house and furniture

HISTOIRE

L ouise et Mary sont meilleures amies. Elles sont aussi **colocataires**. Elles partagent un **appartement** dans centre-ville. Aujourd'hui, elles veulent acheter des **meubles** pour leur **logement**. Louise et Mary sont toutes deux étudiantes. Elles n'ont pas beaucoup d'argent.

« Où pouvons-nous faire les magasins? demande Louise à Mary.

- Nous avons besoin de beaucoup de meubles, dit Mary. Elle s'inquiète pour l'argent.

- Je sais, dit Louise. Nous devons trouver une **bonne affaire**.

- J'ai une idée. Allons au magasin d'occasion! dit Mary.

- Excellente idée! » dit Louise.

Les deux filles vont au magasin d'occasion en voiture. C'est un magasin géant. Le bâtiment est plus grand que dix **maisons**.

Les filles garent la voiture. Le parking est vide.

« Wow, dit Louise. Le magasin est très grand.

- Carrément, dit Mary. Et il n'y a personne ici.

- Nous serons les seules clientes, dit Louise. On peut **faire comme chez nous**. »

Les filles entrent dans le magasin. Le magasin a de tout. À droite, il y a le rayon **cuisine**. Il y a de grands **réfrigérateurs** et de vieux **fours micro-ondes** sur les **étagères**. Il y a des grille-pain de toutes les couleurs. Les prix sont corrects. Un four micro-ondes coûte seulement 10 $.

Tout est une affaire. Les articles sont déjà utilisés et d'occasion. Cependant, Mary et Louise trouvent des articles qu'elles aiment. Il y a plus d'une douzaine de canapés. Mary et Louise ont besoin d'un **canapé.** Elles passent du temps à parler des différents canapés. Mary aime un canapé en cuir brun. Louise aime un grand canapé violet. Elles n'arrivent pas à se décider. Louise voit une chaise violette. Les filles décident de prendre le canapé et la chaise violette pour qu'ils soient assortis. C'est parfait pour leur maison.

« J'ai besoin d'un **lit** pour ma **chambre** », dit Louise.

Les filles vont au rayon chambre à coucher. D'abord, elles passent devant le rayon art.

« Tu sais, nous avons besoin de quelque chose pour les **murs** », dit Louise. Mary est d'accord. Il y a de grands tableaux, de petits tableaux, des **cadres** vides et des photographies dans des cadres. Louise choisit une grande peinture abstraite. Il a des lignes de peinture rouge, bleue et noire.

« Je peux peindre comme ça, dit Mary. On dirait une peinture d'enfant.

- C'est seulement cinq dollars », dit Louise.

- Oh, ok! » dit Mary.

Les filles finissent leurs courses. Louise trouve aussi une **lampe** pour sa chambre. Sa chambre est trop sombre. Mary choisit un **tapis** pour la **salle de bain**. Les filles sont très heureuses. Elles ne dépensent que 100 $ pour tout le mobilier.

« C'est pourquoi faire ses achats au magasin d'occasion est une aubaine, affirme Louise.

- Oui, nous avons **tout sauf l'évier de la cuisine!** » dit Mary.

Mary et Louise organisent une fête dans leur appartement ce soir-là. C'est une fête pour accueillir des amis. Mary et Louise veulent montrer leur nouveau mobilier.

On sonne à la porte. Mary ouvre la **porte**. Nick est le premier à arriver. Nick est l'ami de Mary. Nick est également étudiant. Il étudie l'histoire de l'art.

« Bonjour, mesdames, dit Nick. Merci de m'avoir invité.

- Entre, Nick! » dit Mary. Nick entre dans le **hall d'entrée**. Elle l'embrasse.

« Veux-tu voir nos nouveaux meubles? demande Louise.

- Oui! » dit Nick.

Louise et Mary font visiter l'appartement à Nick. Elles sont contentes du **salon**. Le nouveau canapé, la chaise et la peinture sont superbes.

« Tout cela vient du magasin d'occasion », dit Mary. Elle est fière.

Nick se dirige vers le tableau. « J'aime beaucoup ce tableau, dit-il.

- Moi aussi, dit Louise. Je l'ai choisi.

- Ça me rappelle Jackson Pollock, dit Nick.

- Qui est Jackson Pollock? » demande Mary.

- C'est un peintre très célèbre, dit Nick. Il projette de la peinture sur une toile. Exactement comme celui-ci. » Nick regarde de près la peinture.

« Est-ce signé? » demande-t-il. Louise hoche la tête non. « Regardons derrière alors. »

Ils enlèvent la peinture du cadre et la retournent. Ils sont tous silencieux. Au bas, il y a une signature qui ressemble à « Jackson Pollock ».

« Combien avez-vous payé pour cela? demande Nick.

- Environ cinq dollars, dit Louise.

- Cela vaut probablement au moins 10 millions de dollars », dit Nick. Il est choqué. Mary regarde Louise. Louise regarde Mary.

« Quelqu'un veut-il une coupe de champagne? » dit Mary.

C'est une bonne affaire !

Liste de Vocabulaire

roommates	colocataires
apartment	appartement
furniture	meubles
home	maison
bargain	affaire
thrift store	magasin d'occasion
house	maison
make ourselves at home	faire comme chez nous
kitchen	cuisine
refrigerators	réfrigérateurs
microwaves	micro-ondes
shelves	étagères
toasters	grille-pain
chair	chaise

table	tableau
sofa	canapé
bed	lit
bedroom	chambre à coucher
wall	mur
frame	cadre
lamp	lampe
carpet	tapis
bathroom	salle de bain
everything but the kitchen sink	tout sauf l'évier de cuisine
door	porte
foyer	hall d'entrée
living room	salon

QUESTIONS

1) Pourquoi Mary et Louise vont-elles au magasin d'occasion?

   a) Elles ont besoin d'argent.

   b) Elles ont besoin de meubles, mais n'ont pas beaucoup d'argent.

   c) Elles ont des meubles à vendre.

   d) Elles veulent s'amuser.

2) Pourquoi les prix au magasin d'occasions sont-ils si bas?

   a) C'est la saison des soldes.

   b) Il va fermer.

   c) Les articles ont été utilisés.

   d) Les prix sont normaux et non pas bas.

3) Lequel des articles suivants va dans une cuisine?

a) lit

b) micro-ondes

c) douche

d) canapé

4) Comment Nick en sait-il autant sur le tableau ?

a) C'est un marchand d'art professionnel.

b) Le tableau appartient à Nick.

c) Il étudie l'art.

d) Il a lu un livre.

5) À la fin, Mary et Louise sont...

a) tristes.

b) surprises et riches.

c) en colère contre Nick.

d) trop fatiguées pour faire la fête.

RÉPONSES

1) Pourquoi Mary et Louise vont-elles au magasin d'occasion?

    a) Elles ont besoin d'argent.

2) Pourquoi les prix au magasin d'occasions sont-ils si bas?

    c) Les articles ont été utilisés.

3) Lequel des articles suivants va dans une cuisine?

    b) micro-ondes

4) Comment Nick en sait-il autant sur le tableau ?

    c) Il étudie l'art.

5) À la fin, Mary et Louise sont...

    b) surprises et riches.

Translation of the Story

Thrift Store Bargain

STORY

Louise and Mary are best friends. They are also **roommates**. They share an **apartment** in the center of town. Today they want to shop for **furniture** for their **home**. Louise and Mary are both students. They do not have much money.

"Where can we shop?" Louise asks Mary.

"We need a lot of furniture," Mary says. She is worried about money.

"I know," says Louise. "We need to find a **bargain**."

"I have an idea. Let's go to the thrift store!" says Mary.

"Great idea!" says Louise.

The two girls drive the car to the thrift store. It is a giant store. The building is bigger than ten **houses**.

The girls park the car. The parking lot is empty.

"Wow," says Louise. "The store is very big."

"Totally," says Mary. "And there is nobody here."

"We will be the only people," says Louise. "We can **make ourselves at home.**"

The girls walk into the store. The store has everything. On the right, there is the **kitchen** section. There are tall **refrigerators** and old **microwaves** on the **shelves**. There are **toasters** of all colors. The prices are good. A microwave costs only $10.

Everything is a bargain. The items are used and second-hand. However, Mary and Louise find items that they like. There are more than a dozen sofas. Mary and Louise need a **sofa**. They spend time talking about the different sofas. Mary likes a brown leather sofa. Louise likes a big purple sofa. They cannot decide. Louise sees a purple **chair**. The girls decide to get the purple sofa and chair so that they match. It is perfect for their home.

"I need a **bed** for my **bedroom**," says Louise.

The girls walk to the bedroom area. First, they pass the art section.

"You know, we need something for the **walls**," says Louise. Mary agrees. There are big paintings, small paintings, empty **frames**, and photographs in frames. Louise decides on a big, abstract painting. It has lines of splattered red, blue, and black paint.

"I can paint like that," says Mary. "It looks like a child's painting."

"It's only five dollars," says Louise.

"Oh, ok!" says Mary.

The girls finish shopping. Louise also finds a **lamp** for her bedroom. Her bedroom is too dark.

Mary chooses a **carpet** for the **bathroom**. The girls are very happy. They spend only $100 dollars for all the furniture.

"That is why shopping at the thrift store is a bargain," says Louise.

"Yes, we got **everything but the kitchen sink**!" says Mary.

Mary and Louise have a party in their apartment that night. It is a party to welcome friends. Mary and Louise want to show their new furniture.

The doorbell rings. Mary opens the **door**. Nick is the first to arrive. Nick is Mary's friend. Nick is also a student. He studies art history.

"Hi, ladies," says Nick. "Thank you for inviting me."

"Come in, Nick!" says Mary. Nick steps into the **foyer**. She hugs him.

"Do you want to see our new stuff?" asks Louise.

"Yeah!" says Nick.

Louise and Mary show Nick around the apartment. They are happy with the **living room**. The new sofa, chair and painting looks great.

"All of this is from the thrift store," says Mary. She is proud.

Nick walks up to the painting. "I really like this painting," he says.

"I do too," says Louise. "I chose it."

"It reminds me of Jackson Pollock," says Nick.

"Who is Jackson Pollock?" asks Mary.

"He is a very famous painter," says Nick. "He splashes paint onto canvas. Just like this one." Nick looks closely at the painting.

"Is it signed?" he asks. Louise shakes her head no. "Let's look behind it then."

They take the painting out of the frame and turn it around. They all are quiet. On the bottom is a signature that looks like 'Jackson Pollock'.

"How much did you pay for this?" asks Nick.

"About five dollars," says Louise.

"This is probably worth at least $10 million dollars," says Nick. He is shocked. Mary looks at Louise. Louise looks at Mary.

"Does anyone want a glass of champagne?" says Mary.

Now that is a bargain!

CHAPTER 3
The Goat / common present tense verbs

Ollie se réveille. Le soleil brille. Il se souvient qu'on est samedi. Aujourd'hui, son père ne **travaille** pas. Cela signifie qu'Ollie et son **père** font quelque chose ensemble. Que peuvent-ils faire? Ollie **veut** aller au cinéma. Il veut aussi jouer aux jeux vidéo.

Ollie a 12 ans. Il va à l'école. Le samedi, il ne va pas à l'école. Il **utilise** le samedi pour faire ce qu'il veut. Son père le laisse décider. Ollie veut faire quelque chose d'amusant.

« Papaaaaaaa! » **appelle** Ollie. « **Viens** ici! »

Ollie attend.

Son père entre dans la chambre d'Ollie.

« Aujourd'hui c'est samedi, **dit** Ollie.

- Je **sais**, fils, dit le père d'Ollie.

- Je veux faire quelque chose d'amusant! dit Ollie.

- Moi aussi, dit papa.

- Que pouvons-nous faire? **demande** Ollie.

- Que veux-tu faire ? demande son père.

- Allez au cinéma, dit Ollie.

- Nous allons toujours au cinéma le samedi, dit le père d'Ollie.

- Jouez aux jeux vidéo, dit Ollie.

- Nous jouons à des jeux vidéo tous les jours! dit papa.

- Ok, ok », dit Ollie. Il **réfléchit**. Il se souvient de son enseignant à l'école. Son enseignant **dit** aux élèves de sortir. L'enseignant leur dit que l'air frais est bon. À l'école, ils étudient les animaux. Ollie étudie les animaux de la jungle, les animaux de l'océan et les animaux de la ferme.

Ça y est !

« Papa, allons à la ferme! » dit Ollie. Le père d'Ollie pense que c'est une excellente idée. Il a toujours voulu **voir** et caresser er les animaux de la ferme.

Ils prennent la voiture. Le père d'Ollie conduit pour aller à la campagne. Ils voient un panneau qui dit « Ferme aux animaux ». Ils suivent les panneaux et garent la voiture.

Ollie et son père achètent des tickets pour entrer. Les tickets coûtent 5 $. Ils sortent de la billetterie.

Il y a un grand bâtiment en bois, la ferme. Derrière la ferme, il y a un immense champ. Le champ a des arbres, de l'herbe et des clôtures. Dans chaque clôture, il y a un type d'animal différent. Il y a des centaines d'animaux.

Ollie est enthousiaste. Il voit des poulets, des chevaux, des canards et des cochons. Il les touche et les écoute. Ollie **fait** un bruit à chaque animal. Pour les canards, il dit « coincoin ». Pour les porcs, il dit « groin groin ». Pour les chevaux, il dit « huuu ». Pour les poulets, il dit « cot cot ». Les animaux regardent Ollie.

Passé les animaux dans les cages, Ollie voit un troupeau de moutons. Le père d'Ollie lui dit que les moutons femelles sont appelées brebis. Les moutons mâles sont des béliers. Les bébés moutons sont appelés les agneaux. Les moutons mangent de l'herbe.

« Ils peuvent nous voir, dit papa.

- Mais ils ne nous regardent pas, dit Ollie.

- Les moutons peuvent voir derrière eux. Ils n'ont pas à tourner la tête, dit papa. Le père d'Ollie en sait beaucoup sur les moutons.

« Ils ont coupé la laine des moutons au printemps », dit papa. Il raconte à Ollie comment la laine des moutons devient un chandail, un foulard et d'autres vêtements chauds. Ollie a un pull en laine. Il est chaud.

Ollie et son père marchent dans le champ. L'herbe est verte. Il y a des vaches dans un coin. L'une des vaches mères nourrit un petit veau.

« Tu sais ce que font les vaches, Ollie ? demande papa.

- Bah! Du Lait, dit Ollie.

- C'est exact, dit papa.

Ollie entend un bruit d'animal. Il **prend** la main de son père. Ils marchent vers le son. Ils arrivent à une clôture. Ils **trouvent** une chèvre. La chèvre a ses cornes coincées dans la clôture. La chèvre est assise sur le sol. Elle ne bouge pas. Ses cornes sont entre les plaques de bois et elle ne peut pas bouger. Ollie et son père **regardent** la chèvre.

« Je me sens tellement mal pour la chèvre, dit Ollie. Elle semble triste.

- Pauvre gars! dit papa.

- Elle a l'air si triste, dit Ollie.

- Nous pouvons l'aider, dit papa.

- Oui! » dit Ollie.

Ils se rapprochent de la chèvre. Ollie est nerveux. Papa dit de ne pas s'inquiéter. Les cornes sont coincées et la chèvre ne leur fera pas de mal. Ollie regarde dans les yeux de la chèvre. La chèvre **a besoin** d'aide. Ollie parle à la chèvre. Il **essaie** de faire des sons doux. Il veut garder la chèvre calme.

Le père d'Ollie essaie de déplacer les cornes. Il essaie la corne droite. Il essaie la corne gauche. Elles ne bougent pas. Après dix minutes, ils **abandonnent**.

« Je n'y arrive pas, dit le père d'Ollie.

- Es-tu sûr? demande Ollie.

- Les cornes sont coincées, dit papa.

- Que faisons-nous? » demande Ollie.

Autour de la chèvre, il y a de la boue. Il n'y a plus d'herbe. Le père d'Ollie ramasse de l'herbe et l'apporte à la chèvre. La chèvre mange l'herbe. La chèvre a l'air affamée. L'herbe a disparu. Ollie prend plus d'herbe pour la donner à la chèvre. Ils caressent la chèvre pendant quelques minutes. La chèvre semble reconnaissante.

« Prévenons le propriétaire, dit papa.

- Oui, dit Ollie. Peut-être qu'ils peuvent l'aider. »

Ollie et son père vont à la billetterie. La billetterie est un petit bâtiment à l'entrée. Un homme y travaille. Ollie et son père rentrent à l'intérieur.

« Bonjour, monsieur, dit le père d'Ollie.

- Comment puis-je vous aider? demande l'homme.

- Il y a une chèvre — dit le père d'Ollie.

L'homme interrompt le père d'Ollie. Il agite la main. Il a l'air de s'ennuyer. « Oui, nous savons. »

« Vous savez pour la chèvre ? demande Ollie.

- La chèvre coincée dans la clôture ? demande l'homme.

- Oui! disent Ollie et son père.

- Oh oui, c'est Patty, dit l'homme. Elle peut se libérer quand elle veut. Elle aime juste attirer l'attention. »

Ollie regarde son père d'un air surpris. Ollie et son père rient.

« Patty, quelle chèvre! » dit Ollie.

RÉSUMÉ

Ollie se réveille un samedi. Lui et son père décident de faire quelque chose d'amusant. Ils vont dans une ferme pour voir des animaux. Ils voient et caressent de nombreux animaux : des vaches, des chevaux, des moutons et plus encore. Ils se promènent dans la ferme. C'est une belle journée. Ils trouvent une chèvre coincée dans une clôture. Ils essaient d'aider la chèvre. La chèvre a ses cornes coincées. Ils la nourrissent d'herbe. Ollie et son père vont chercher de l'aide. L'homme à la billetterie les écoute. Il leur dit que la chèvre aime tromper les gens pour attirer l'attention. Ollie et son père rient.

Liste de Vocabulaire

to work	au travail
to do	faire
to want	vouloir
to go	aller
to use	utiliser
to call	appeler
to come	venir
to say	dire
to know	savoir
to ask	demander
to think	penser
to tell	dire
to see	voir
to become	devenir
to make	de faire

to take	prendre
to find	trouver
to feel	sentir
to look	chercher
to get	obtenir
to need	besoin
to try	essayer
to give	donner

QUESTIONS

1) Que décident Ollie et son père de faire le samedi?

    a) aller au cinéma

    b) aller à la ferme

    c) jouer à des jeux vidéo

    d) aller à l'école

2) Quel animal le père d'Ollie connaît-il le mieux?

    a) les moutons

    b) les cochons

    c) la girafe

    d) la vache

3) Qu'arrive-t-il à la chèvre?

    a) elle se cache

    b) elle mange

c) elle est coincée

d) elle est en colère

4) Que font Ollie et son père pour la chèvre?

a) ils la libèrent

b) ils lui donnent de l'herbe et la caressent

c) ils appellent la police pour l'attraper

d) ils lui font un bisou

5) Que fait Patty?

a) elle quitte la ferme

b) elle mange des ordures

c) elle se rend à la billetterie

d) elle fait semblant d'être coincée pour attirer l'attention

RÉPONSES

1) Que décide Ollie et son père de faire le samedi?

b) aller à la ferme

2) Quel animal le père d'Ollie connaît-il le mieux?

a) les moutons

3) Qu'arrive-t-il à la chèvre?

c) elle est coincée

4) Que font Ollie et son père pour la chèvre?

b) ils lui donnent de l'herbe et la caressent

5) Que fait Patty?

d) elle fait semblant d'être coincée pour attirer l'attention

Translation of the Story

The Goat

Ollie wakes up. The sun is shining. He remembers: it is Saturday. Today his dad does not **work**. That means Ollie and his dad **do** something together. What can they do? Ollie **wants** to go to the movies. He also wants to play video games.

Ollie is twelve years old. He goes to school. Saturday he does not go to school. He **uses** Saturday to do what he wants. His dad lets him decide. So Ollie wants to do something fun.

"Daaaaaad!" **calls** Ollie. "**Come** here!"

Ollie waits.

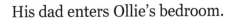

His dad enters Ollie's bedroom.

"Today is Saturday," **says** Ollie.

"I **know**, son," says Ollie's dad.

"I want to do something fun!" says Ollie.

"Me too," says Dad.

"What can we do?" **asks** Ollie.

"What do you want to do?" asks his dad.

"Go to the movies," says Ollie.

"We always go to the movies on Saturday," says Ollie's dad.

"Play video games," says Ollie.

"We play video games everyday!" says Dad.

"Ok, ok," says Ollie. He **thinks**. He remembers his teacher at school. His teacher **tells** the students to go outside. The teacher tells them the fresh air is good. At school, they study animals. Ollie learns about animals in the jungle, animals in the ocean, and animals on farms.

That's it!

"Dad, let's go to a farm!" says Ollie. Ollie's dad thinks that is a great idea. He has always wanted to **see** and touch farm animals.

They take the car. Ollie's dad drives to the countryside. They see a sign that says "Animal Farm". They follow the signs and park the car.

Ollie and his dad buy tickets to enter. Tickets cost $5. They leave the ticket office. There is a big wooden building, the farmhouse. Behind the farmhouse, there is a huge field. The field has trees, grass, and fences. In each fence is a different type of animal. There are hundreds of animals.

Ollie is excited. He sees chickens, horses, ducks, and pigs. He touches them and listens to them. Ollie **makes** a sound to each animal. To the ducks, he says "quack". To the pigs, he says "oink". To the horses, he says "nay". To the chickens, he says "bok bok". The animals stare at Ollie.

Past the animals in cages, Ollie sees a flock of sheep. Ollie's dad tells him that female sheep are called ewes. Male sheep are rams. Baby sheep are called lambs. The sheep are eating grass.

"They can see us," says Dad.

"But they are not looking at us," says Ollie.

"Sheep can see behind themselves. They don't have to turn their heads," says Dad. Ollie's dad knows a lot about sheep.

"They cut the hair on the sheep in spring," says Dad. He tells Ollie how the sheep's wool **becomes** sweaters, scarves and other warm clothing. Ollie has a sweater made of wool. It is warm.

Ollie and his dad walk around the field. The grass is green. There are cows in a corner. One of the mother cows feeds a baby calf.

"You know what cows make, Ollie?" asks Dad.

"Duh! Milk!" says Ollie.

"That's right," says Dad.

Ollie hears an animal sound. He **takes** his dad's hand. They walk towards the sound. They come to a fence. They **find** a goat. The goat has horns stuck in the fence. The goat sits on the ground. It does not move. Its horns are between the wood and it can't move. Ollie and his dad **look** at the goat.

"I feel so bad for the goat," says Ollie. She seems sad.

"Poor guy!" says Dad.

"He looks so sad," says Ollie.

"We can help him," Dad says.

"Yeah!" says Ollie.

They get close to the goat. Ollie is nervous. Dad says not to worry. The horns are stuck and the goat will not hurt them. Ollie looks into the eyes of the goat. The goat **needs** help. Ollie talks to the goat. He **tries** to make soft sounds. He wants to keep the goat calm.

Ollie's dad tries to move the horns. He tries the right horn. He tries the left horn. They don't move. After ten minutes, they **give up**.

"I can't do it," says Ollie's dad.

"Are you sure?" asks Ollie.

"The horns are stuck," says Dad.

"What do we do?" asks Ollie.

The area around the goat is mud. There is no grass left. Ollie's dad takes some grass from the ground and brings it to the goat. The goat eats the grass.

The goat looks hungry. The grass is gone. Ollie gets more grass to take to the goat. They pet the goat for a few minutes. The goat seems grateful.

"Let's tell the owner," says Dad.

"Yeah," says Ollie. "Maybe they can help her."

Ollie and his dad go to the ticket office. The ticket office is a small building at the entrance. A man works there. Ollie and his dad go inside.

"Hello, sir," says Ollie's dad.

"How can I help you?" asks the man.

"There's a goat—" says Ollie's dad.

The man interrupts Ollie's dad. He waves his hand. He looks bored. "Yeah, we know."

"You know about the goat?" asks Ollie.

"The goat stuck in the fence?" asks the man.

"Yes!" say Ollie and his dad.

"Oh yes, that's Patty," says the man. "She can get herself out whenever she wants. She just likes the attention."

Ollie **gives** his dad a surprised look. Ollie and his dad laugh.

"Patty, what a goat!" Ollie says.

CONCLUSION

You did it!

You finished a whole book in a brand-new language. That in and of itself is quite the accomplishment, isn't it?

Congratulate yourself on time well spent and a job well done. Now that you've finished the book, you have familiarized yourself with over 500 new vocabulary words, comprehended the heart of 3 short stories, and listened to loads of dialogue unfold, all without going anywhere!

Charlemagne said "To have another language is to possess a second soul." After immersing yourself in this book, you are broadening your horizons and opening a whole new path for yourself.

Have you thought about how much you know now that you did not know before? You've learned everything from how to greet and how to express your emotions to basics like colors and place words. You can tell time and ask question. All without opening a schoolbook. Instead, you've cruised through fun, interesting stories and possibly listened to them as well.

Perhaps before you weren't able to distinguish meaning when you listened to French. If you used the audiobook, we bet you can now pick out meanings and words when you hear someone speaking. Regardless, we are sure you have taken an important step to being more fluent. You are well on your way!

Best of all, you have made the essential step of distinguishing in your mind the idea that most often hinders people studying a new language. By approaching French through our short stories and dialogs, instead of formal lessons with just grammar and vocabulary, you are no longer in the 'learning' mindset. Your approach is much more similar to an osmosis, focused on speaking and using the language, which is the end goal, after all!

So, what's next?

This is just the first of five books, all packed full of short stories and dialogs, covering essential, everyday French that will ensure you master the basics. You can find the rest of the books in the series, as well as a whole host of other resources, at LearnLikeNatives.com. Simply add the book to your library to take the next step in your language learning journey. If you are ever in need of new ideas or direction, refer to our 'Speak Like a Native' eBook, available to you for free at LearnLikeNatives.com, which clearly outlines practical steps you can take to continue learning any language you choose.

We also encourage you to get out into the real world and practice your French. You have a leg up on most beginners, after all—instead of pure textbook learning, you have been absorbing the sound and soul of the language. Do not underestimate the foundation you have built reviewing the chapters of this book. Remember, no one feels 100% confident when they speak with a native speaker in another language.

One of the coolest things about being human is connecting with others. Communicating with someone in their own language is a wonderful gift. Knowing the language turns you into a local and opens up your world. You will see the reward of learning languages for many years to come, so keep that practice up!. Don't let your fears stop you from taking the chance to use your French. Just give it a try, and remember that you will make mistakes. However, these mistakes will teach you so much, so view every single one as a small victory! Learning is growth.

Don't let the quest for learning end here! There is so much you can do to continue the learning process in an organic way, like you did with this book. Add another book from Learn Like a Native to your library. Listen to French talk radio. Watch some of the great French films. Put on the latest CD from Edith Piaf. Take cooking lessons in French. Whatever you do, don't stop because every little step you take counts towards learning a new language, culture, and way of communicating.

www.LearnLikeNatives.com

Learn Like a Native is a revolutionary **language education brand** that is taking the linguistic world by storm. Forget boring grammar books that never get you anywhere, Learn Like a Native teaches you languages in a fast and fun way that actually works!

As an international, multichannel, language learning platform, we provide **books, audio guides and eBooks** so that you can acquire the knowledge you need, swiftly and easily.

Our **subject-based learning**, structured around real-world scenarios, builds your conversational muscle and ensures you learn the content most relevant to your requirements.
Discover our tools at ***LearnLikeNatives.com***.

When it comes to learning languages, we've got you covered!

CPSIA information can be obtained
at www.ICGtesting.com
Printed in the USA
BVHW092032110621
609349BV00005B/1619